Nail Art

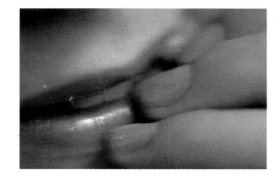

Sherri Haab

KLUTZ

KLUTZ. is an independent publishing company staffed entirely by real human beings. We began our corporate life back in 1977 in a Palo Alto, California garage that we shared with a Chevrolet Impala. Back then, founders John Cassidy, Darrell Hack and BC Rimbeaux were all students and one of the founding principles was thusly stated: be in and out of business by the end of summer vacation.

So much for that plan.

Plan B? Create the best-written, best-looking, most imaginative books in the world. Be honest and fair in all our dealings. Work hard to make every day feel like the first day of summer vacation.

We aim high.

We'd love to hear your comments about this book.

Write us.

KLUTZ.
455 Portage Avenue
Palo Alto, CA 94306

Additional Copies:

Give us a call at (650) 857-0888 and we'll help track down your nearest Klutz retailer. Should they be out of stock, additional copies of this book as well as the entire library of 100% Klutz certified books, are available in the Klutz Catalogue. See the last page for details.

Thanks To:

Thea Lorentzen
for the great idea.

And To:

Judy Bramsen
Jacqueline Lee
Jill Taylor
Laura Torres
Kathy Summers
Annette Wimsatt
Pam Kidd
Marilyn Green
Joel Eastman
Jeff Hill
and all the Klutzes

Designs

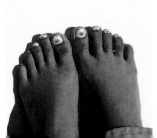

Getting  Started

Nail painting is a lot like facepainting (multiplied by 10 of course). The steps are just as easy.

1. Gather up a few toothpicks (or something like them) to use for fine line work. Get a water-based felt tip marker for making tiny dots. For spills, set the book down on a sheet or two of newspaper.

2. The paints will dry in a minute or so unless you lay them on extra extra thick. Wait for each color to dry before you paint right up next to it or on top of it.

3. Flip to a design you'd like to try, take a deep breath and start right in. Use the brush in the bottle for painting broad areas. Use the toothpick for careful line work.

4. To make new colors, do a little mixing on a clean sheet of scrap paper.

5. What's the One Big Secret to creating fingernail masterpieces? All our experts agree. Patience and a steady hand. Beyond that, no artistic talent required.

A Few Words About Our Paints

Our nail colors have been formulated exclusively for us. Commercial nail polishes are solvent-based and require the use of nail polish remover. Ours do not. They are water-based and non-toxic. When you're done with your designs, you may peel or wash off the colors with soap and water.

If you spill, use warm soapy water immediately to minimize staining.

Safety: Don't apply the paints to open wounds. Don't eat them or give them to anyone who might do it by mistake. If a rash develops after use, discontinue and consult a physician.

Working with paint

1. Shake paint well before using. Always paint your fingernails or toenails over an old newspaper or magazine. Let the paint dry before touching clothing or walking on carpet.

2. Mistakes on your nail or skin can be washed off with water.

3. Remember to use the paint in a thin layer or small drops. Too much paint takes a long time to dry.

4. The paint can ruin the brush if you let it dry. Wash the brush in-between mixing colors and dry the brush by dabbing it on a paper towel.

5. Always re-cap paint so that it won't dry out.

Mixing colors

If you think the polish needs to be thinner, add just a couple drops of water
to the bottle, screw the cap on tightly, and shake well.

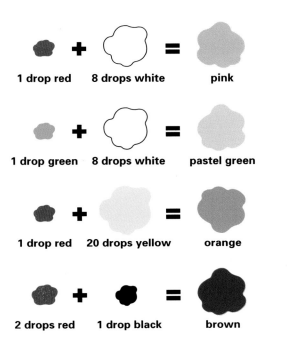

1 drop red **+** 8 drops white **=** pink

1 drop green **+** 8 drops white **=** pastel green

1 drop red **+** 20 drops yellow **=** orange

2 drops red **+** 1 drop black **=** brown

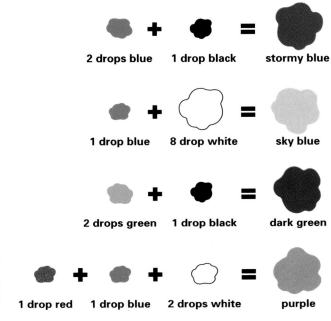

2 drops blue **+** 1 drop black **=** stormy blue

1 drop blue **+** 8 drop white **=** sky blue

2 drops green **+** 1 drop black **=** dark green

1 drop red **+** 1 drop blue **+** 2 drops white **=** purple

Clear Nail Polish

If you're over 12 years old, you can use clear nail polish (from the drugstore) to make your design last longer. Start with a coat of clear polish; let it dry, then paint your design. Make sure the design is dry before adding a top coat of clear polish. It's always a good idea to keep real nail polish (clear or not) away from small children.

How to paint your nails

1. Dip the brush into the paint. Drag the brush against the opening of the bottle to keep from getting too much paint on your nail. This also helps to keep the paint from accidentally dripping.

 2. Paint a strip down the center of your nail, starting at the cuticle and brushing to the tip.

3. Paint down each side of your nail, first one side and then the other.

4. Recap the bottle tightly and let your nails dry before touching anything.

5. A blow dryer can be used to speed up the drying of your nails.

Working with glitter

1. Fold a piece of paper in half to catch the glitter under your nails.

2. Sprinkle the glitter over wet polish, paint or white glue. Shake off the extra glitter over the paper.

3. Use the fold of the paper to pour the glitter back into the container.

4. Re-cap the glitter quickly to avoid spills.

Working with jewels, eyes and beads

1. Make a small dot of white glue on your nail with a toothpick. Place the jewel on the glue and press it gently. Let the glue dry.

2. You can glue wiggle eyes, small beads and sequins onto your painted nails.

How to make basic shapes

Circles:

1. Dab a small blob of paint onto scrap paper. Dip the end of a paintbrush into paint. Hold the brush straight up and down and make a dot of paint on your nail.

2. Use a toothpick to make tinier dots.

3. To make large circles, follow Step 1 and dot the paint onto your nail. Swirl the paint around in a circular motion with the end of the brush until the circle is the size you want.

Teardrop shape:

1. Dip the end of your paintbrush into paint and dot it onto your nail. Use a toothpick to pull paint to a point. (This shape can be used for flower petals, leaves, animal ears and hearts.) Use a toothpick for both steps on smaller designs.

Lines:

1. Dip a toothpick into paint and draw lines on your nail. You may need to re-dip the toothpick to grab more paint as you need it. The more paint you pick up with the toothpick, the thicker the line will be.

Layers of paint:

1. Some designs use layers of paint, such as a solid painted nail with a design on it (example: eyeball on an eye). It is important to let each layer dry before painting over it. This will prevent smearing paint or designs that take too long to dry.

2. If you have a dry layer of paint and you make a mistake while painting a design on top, you can use a damp cotton ball or tissue to wipe the paint off without disturbing the dry layer underneath. If you want to start over completely, let the paint dry and peel the paint off of your nail.

Sunflowers

 Paint a brown dot in the center of your nail.

Add six yellow dots around the center one.

Try other color combinations for a mixed bouquet.

12

Make other flowers by using a toothpick to change the petal shapes.

Flower Vine

Use a toothpick to draw a wavy green line. Add green dots for leaves. Let the paint dry.

For each flower, dot five small petals in a circle. Let dry.

Add a dot in the center of each flower.

Make two dots at the top of your nail. With a toothpick, drag the wet paint down toward the center.

Make two dots at the bottom of your nail.

Drag those wet dots up toward the center. Let the paint dry.

Use a toothpick to draw a thin line of paint to make the body and tiny antennae. Decorate the wings with small dots of paint.

Butterflies

bumble

Bees

①

Paint your nail yellow. Let it dry.

②

Paint a black stripe across the top.

③

Use a toothpick to add two thin stripes and two dots for eyes.

Ladybug

①

Paint your nail red. Let it dry.

②

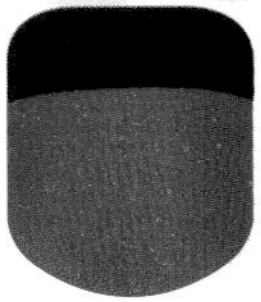

Paint a black stripe across the top.

③

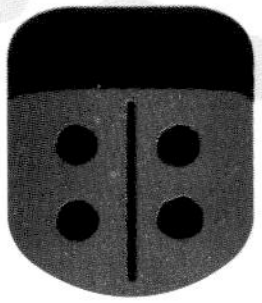

Add four small black dots and a thin black line.

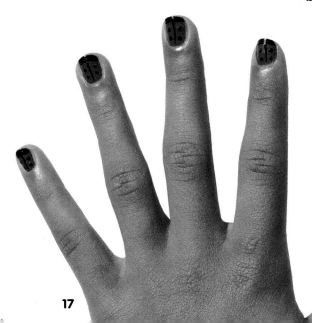

17

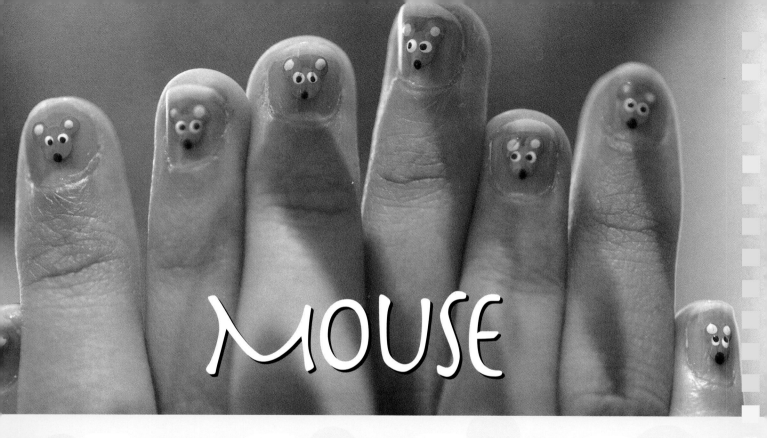

MOUSE

Make a large blue dot in the center of your nail.

Add two smaller dots for the ears. Let the paint dry.

Use a toothpick to make two small white dots for eyes. Let the dots dry.

Add black eyeballs and nose, plus two pinks dots in ears.

LittLe PIGs

Paint your nail pale pink. Let it dry.

Mix a darker pink by adding more red. Make a large dot of dark pink in the center. Let it dry.

Paint two small white dots for eyes.

Use a felt tip pen to add nostrils, eyeballs and ears.

fish

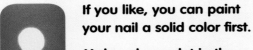
If you like, you can paint your nail a solid color first.

Make a large dot in the center of your nail.

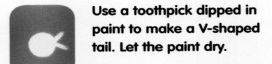
Use a toothpick dipped in paint to make a V-shaped tail. Let the paint dry.

For the eye, make a small white dot with a toothpick. Let it dry, then add a tiny black dot.

Use a toothpick to add tiny dots for bubbles.

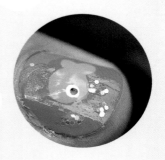

More Nail Art for You to Try

Letters

M

Use a toothpick to draw letters
on your nails. For more colorful letters,
add dots of different colors.

cow spots

Paint your nail white.
Let it dry, then add
irregular black dots.

s o l i d
COLORS

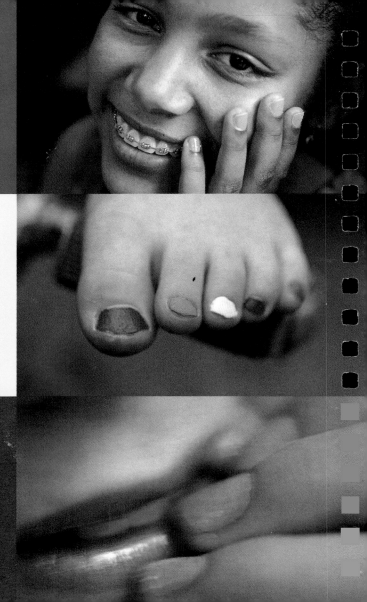

For extra sparkle, paint your nail a color and sprinkle it with glitter while paint is still wet.

Paint your nail a solid color. Let it dry. Add wavy lines with a toothpick.

wavy stripes

triangles

1

2

3

Follow these pictures.
Let paint dry between
each step.

French
manicure

Paint a diagonal stroke of white over the left tip of your nail.

Repeat on the right tip, overlapping strokes in the middle.

Ice Cream Cones

Use a toothpick to paint a yellow cone. Let it dry.

Add three dots of your favorite flavor.

Draw lines with a toothpick.

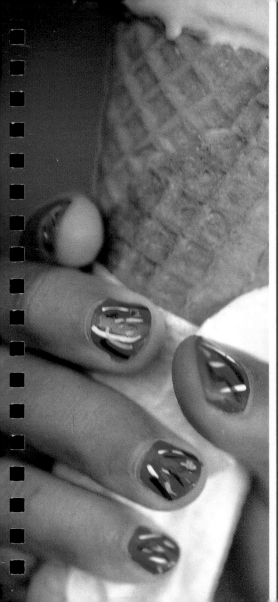

FIREWORKS

Paint your nail dark blue or black. Let it dry. Dot on some bright colors. Drag the dots with a toothpick while they are still wet.

HEARTS

Put a small red dot on left.

Drag it down to a point.

Put second dot on right.

Drag it down so points meet.

Ghosts & Goblins

Use SCARY colors of polish to paint SCARY nails. Witches, pumpkins, monsters, ghosts, bats, tombstones, ghouls, mummies, cats, etc.

Pumpkin
1. Paint your nail orange. Let it dry.
2. Add black triangle eyes and a squiggly mouth.

Ghoul
1. Paint your nail solid black. Let it dry.
2. Add small white dots for eyes. Let the paint dry.
3. Add tiny black dots for eyes.

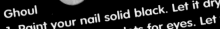

Ghost
1. Paint your nail solid white. Let it dry.
2. Add black eyes and mouth.

Skull
1. Paint a large white dot with a flat bottom. Let it dry.
2. Add tiny black dots for eyes and nose.

Cat
1. Make two large black dots, one above the other.
2. Draw two triangles for ears and a curved line for a tail.

33

DOGS

& PAWS

 Paint your nail a solid color. Let it dry.

 Make three large dots.

 Add three small dots above each big dot.

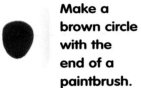 Make a brown circle with the end of a paintbrush.

 Use a tooth-pick to paint black ears and a dot for a nose.

 Use a clean point on a toothpick to make two dots of black for eyes.

snake

Make a dot of green paint on your nail for the snake's head.

Paint a line of green paint from the head across the other nails for the body. Let it dry.

Make a white dot for the eye, with a smaller black dot in the center.

Use a toothpick to paint a red tongue.

fruit

GRAPES:
Make a row of three purple dots at the top of your nail.

Add a row of two dots beneath them.

Add one last dot at the bottom. Let the paint dry.

For the leaf, make a green dot at the top of the grapes. Use a toothpick to pull the dot into a teardrop shape. Use the leftover paint on your toothpick to make a small stem.

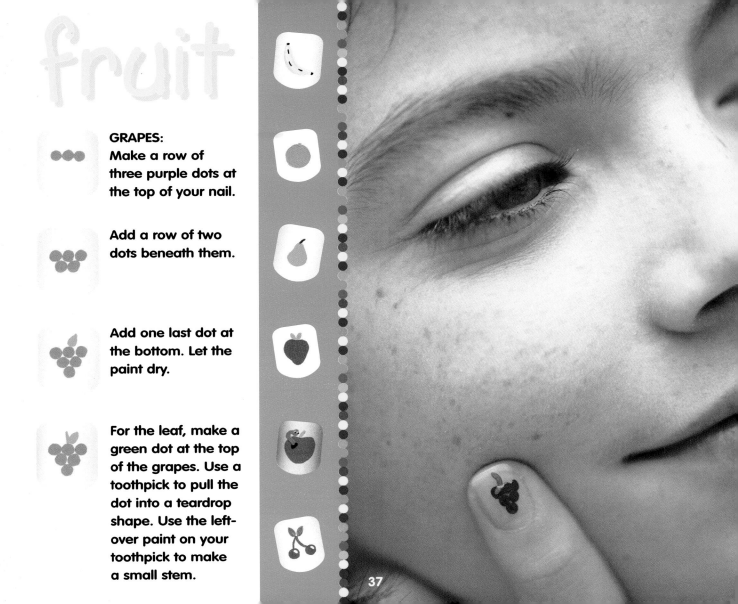

More Nail Art for You to Try

SPRING

Paint your nail a solid color. Let it dry.

Add rows of dots.

Use a toothpick to draw wavy lines.

BUNNY:

Put a large white dot in the center of your nail.

For the ears, make two smaller white dots at the top of your nail. While they're still wet, use a toothpick to drag the dots down to touch the head. Now let everything dry.

Use a pink felt tip pen to make nose and centers of ears. Use a black felt tip pen to add eyes and whiskers.

CHICK:

Paint your nail yellow and let it dry.

Paint the bottom of your nail white.

Dot eyes on with black polish. Make a small orange triangle for a beak.

earth

Paint a big blue dot in the center of your nail. Let it dry.

 Add green continents.

peace

Paint a big color circle in the center of your nail. Let it dry. Use a toothpick to paint a color peace sign on the circle.

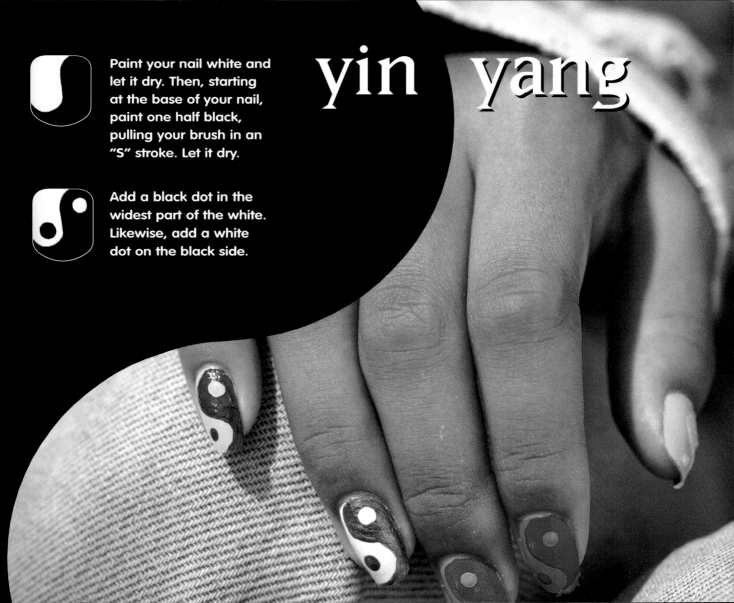

yin yang

Paint your nail white and let it dry. Then, starting at the base of your nail, paint one half black, pulling your brush in an "S" stroke. Let it dry.

Add a black dot in the widest part of the white. Likewise, add a white dot on the black side.

Moon & pLanets

Use a toothpick to make a "C" shape on your nail. Make a second stroke of paint to fatten up the "C" to look like a moon.

Make a large circle in the center of your nail. Let it dry. Use a toothpick to paint a ring around the planet.

Make a ring of dots on your nail. Use a toothpick to pull the dots out to points, while the polish is still wet. Let it dry. Make a large dot for the center.

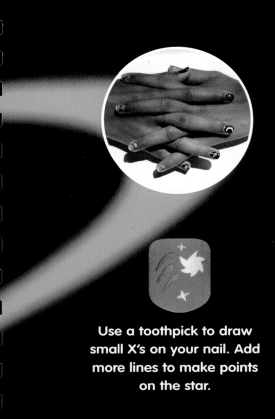

Use a toothpick to draw small X's on your nail. Add more lines to make points on the star.

& stars

POLKA DOTS

dice

Paint your nail
a solid color.
Let the paint dry.

Make dots of
contrast color. Use
the end of your
paintbrush to make
medium-to-large
dots. Use a toothpick
to make tiny dots.

Paint your nail
solid white. Let it dry.
Add black dots.

Use a toothpick to draw a pink square in the center of your nail. Let it dry, then add three lighter pink lines.

 For a candle, draw a blue line with a toothpick.

 Add a dot of yellow for flame.

Birthday
Party

teddy bears

Make a large brown dot in the center of your nail.

Add two smaller dots for ears. Let the paint dry.

With a toothpick, add a small pink dot in the center of each ear. Make a dot of pink for each cheek.

Use a toothpick to make tiny black dots for eyes and nose.

49

1.
Paint your
nail blue.
Let it dry.

2.
Put a large white
dot in the center.
Let it dry.

Baseballs

3.
Use a
toothpick to
make black
stitches.

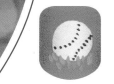

4.
Add grass
with a toothpick
if you've hit a
ground ball.

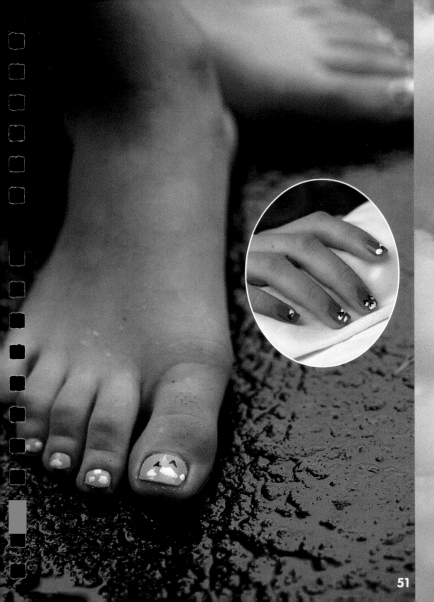

CLOUDS

Paint your nail sky blue
and let it dry. Then dab
on some white clouds.
Let this dry.

Draw black birds
with a toothpick.

STRIPES

1. Paint your nail a solid color. Let it dry.

2. Add contrast stripes with a toothpick.

Or, paint one fat stripe.

No need to stick to straight lines!

MARBLED

Work quickly, while paint is wet! Draw three lines of paint on your nail.

Draw two lines of contrast color between the first lines.

Zigzag back and forth across the lines with a toothpick. Swirl paint over any uncovered areas of your nail.

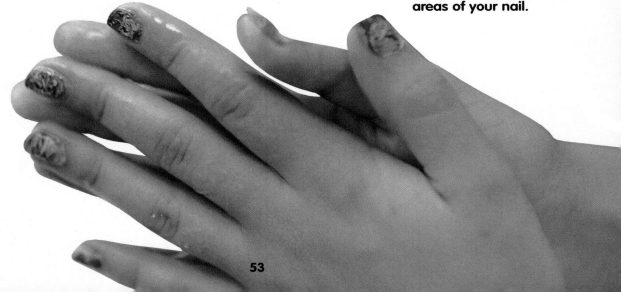

Winter

HOLLY:
Dip a toothpick in green paint and draw a wave shape on one side of your nail.

Make the same shape, upside down, right under the first line. Draw the lines close, with no space between them.

Make another leaf the same way on the other side of your nail. Use a toothpick to make a small red dot under the leaves.

TREE:
Draw six small green dots in a triangle as shown. Let this dry, then add a small red dot at the bottom.

More Nail Art for You to Try

Credits

Book printed in Singapore.
Box made in Taiwan.
Nail colors made
in USA.

ISBN 1-57054-111-6

**Book Design and
Graphic Production:**

Kevin Plottner
MaryEllen Podgorski

Photography:

Thomas Heinser

Illustrations:

Oscar Castillo
Sara Boore

Models: Jocelyn Woolworth, Helen Woolworth, Catherine Woods, Laura Wolfson, Alexandria Viramontes, Hilary Thorndike, Keating Simons, Betsy Sikes, Ashley Siebert, Liensa Rouse, Evanne Riskas, Mandy Raack, Erika Oda, Katie Niner, Gretchen Mueller, Ali Marchese, Liz Lorig, Thea Lorentzen, Luke Lorentzen, Claire Lorentzen, Rachel Kingston, Sarah Kiernan, Erika Gray, Dianne Esber, Katie Daley, Heidi Bennion, Byrdie Bell, Sonia Baca, Nadia Baca, Myuki Arikawa. • **Casting:** Sheila Wolfson, Darrell Lorentzen. • **Photography:** Glitter, pg. 9, Mark Hundley. Butterflies, pg. 15, Tom Stack. Honeybee, pg. 16, by Phillip and Karen Smith, © Tony Stone Worldwide. Ladybug, pg. 17, Tom Stack. Ice cream cone, pg. 30, Mark Hundley. Costumes, pg. 32, Peter Fox. Candy, pg. 33, Mark Hundley. Dog, pg. 34, Peter Fox. Planets, pg. 45 NASA. Cake and kids, pg. 48, Peter Fox. Lights, pg. 54, Mark Hundley.

More Great Books from Klutz

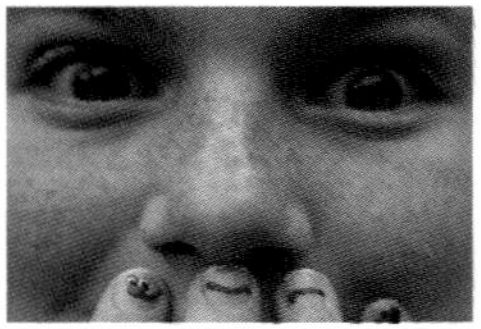

Beads

Boondoggle

The Buck Book

Cat's Cradle

The Incredible Clay Book

Kid's Cooking

Face Painting

Hair

KidSongs

Make Believe

Shadow Games

String Games

Watercolor for the Artistically Undiscovered

Plus 50 others...

KLUTZ®

455 Portage Avenue
Palo Alto, CA 94306

We hope you enjoyed reading NAIL ART as much as we enjoyed writing it! If you want our **FREE** Catalogue, just answer this **lengthy** questionnaire. Grab the nearest pen, fill in the blanks, throw on some postage, and send it our way.

Who are you?

Name: _____

Address: _____

City: _____ State: _____ Zip: _____

How did you first hear about this book? _____

Draw a picture of yourself here ↘

Tell us what you think of this book:

_____

_____

_____

_____

_____

_____

❶ **Tear out**
❷ **Fill in**
❸ **Add stamp**
❹ **Mail**
❺ **Wait impatiently**

What would you like us to write a book about? _____

❏ Check this box If you want us to send you The Klutz Catalogue

NAIL ART